THE SPIRIT OF
NEW FOREST PONIES

MIKE READ

HALSGROVE

First published in Great Britain in 2008

British Library Cataloguing-in-Publication Data
A CIP record for this title is available from the British Library

ISBN 978 1 84114 730 7

HALSGROVE
Halsgrove House
Ryelands Industrial Estate
Bagley Road, Wellington
Somerset TA21 9PZ
Tel: 01823 653777
Fax: 01823 216796
email: sales@halsgrove.com
website: www.halsgrove.com

Printed and bound by Grafiche Flaminia, Italy

Introduction

New Forest ponies are not wild animals. Each pony is owned by someone who lives in a Forest property to which Commoning Rights belong. The 'Right of Pasture' allows Commoners to run ponies (and other animals) on the Forest. Pony deaths on Forest roads are still a problem, despite the 40mph speed limits, and result in considerable financial loss for the Commoner(s) concerned. Each pony is an individual just as we humans are. Most are docile and relaxed while a few can be a little nervous. Some will approach you but it is against the local by-laws to feed them. In general, they make excellent, sure-footed riding mounts.

The constant browsing and grazing by the ponies has resulted in them being called the 'Architects of the New Forest'. Without the ponies, one has to wonder if the area would have remained so important for wildlife and if it would ever have been designated as a National Park. The breed as a whole has an irreplaceable presence that truly reflects the New Forest. Without the ponies and their spirit, the New Forest would certainly be a much poorer place for us to visit.

Foals stay close to their mothers as they are 'drifted' towards a pound.

Opposite: Agisters and Commoners ride together smiling at the end of a successful drift.

A group of ponies in fine condition after a good summer's grazing.

Foals continue to suckle for as long as a mare will allow.

Ponies galloping beside the road may turn in any direction so beware if you are driving nearby!

Some ponies set off at a gallop for no apparent reason.
Perhaps this one heard some relative calling in the distance.

Opposite: A good sheen on this animal's coat shows it is in fine condition.

A group of ponies goes dashing past an idyllic Forest
cottage during a drift; a good time to be indoors!

Riders and helpers discuss plans at the start of a drift.

The leading grey mare makes a break to avoid the pound
while other ponies head in the right direction.

A long mane certainly helps to keep the flies away from a pony's eyes.

When ponies are within a pound they are not able to keep clear
of aggressive biting but this rarely results in any injury. The
flattened ears show either aggression or defensive nervousness.

Even grey ponies can be difficult to see at night so many are now sporting
reflective collars to help reduce the risk of night-time accidents.
Remember that not all ponies will be side on or facing you at night!

Discarded litter can be a real
problem for the Forest's ponies.
Plastic can choke while tin cans and
broken bottles can seriously maim.
Please take your litter home.

An intelligent looking mare
trotting across Ober Heath.

Mutual grooming – you scratch my back and I'll scratch yours.

A young foal rests close to its feeding mother.

Opposite: New Forest ponies come in a variety of colours
but this does not include piebald or skewbald.

When foals of this age get together there can often be fun and frolics.

Worn out from a few minutes of fun, this foal returns to its
mother for some comforting company.

A grey mare and her growing foal graze in the early morning
as the sun breaks through the mist at Fletcher's Green.

The woodland will provide shade when feeding in the glade is completed.

Two ponies feed beneath magnificent beech trees in Mark Ash Wood.

Hey, mum, look at this
funny photographer!

An animal with the usual intelligent
yet friendly appearance of a New
Forest Pony – but an unusually
shaped white star.

There are numerous ponds, pools and streams from which ponies can drink.

Overleaf: Ponies graze on Backley Green as the sun
sets to end another glorious day in the New Forest.

This pony seemed fairly relaxed as it trotted past me...

but as the mare and foal in front of her began trotting faster, she kicked up her heels…

...and then went galloping off.

Gorse can be difficult to eat but during the winter months it gives the ponies lots of vitamins and minerals lacking in the grasses.

Holly also provides the same extra nutrients needed to remain healthy through the winter. If you can't get your children to eat their greens, show them these two pictures!

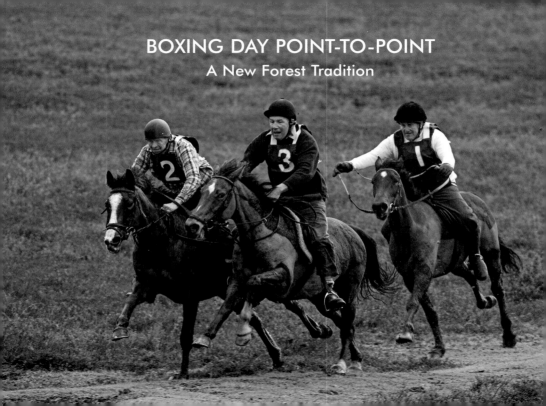

BOXING DAY POINT-TO-POINT
A New Forest Tradition

A muddy, water-filled ditch proves no obstacle for No. 5.

Opposite: Three competitors battle it out for first place in a 2005 Veterans' race at the Boxing Day point-to-point.

A fine leap…

…and the finish line is in sight.

Opposite page:
A mud-splattered competitor completes
a point-to-point course.

Left: Gail Meaker nears the finish line to win the Novice New Forest Ponies race in the 2007 Boxing Day point-to-point.

Below: Ears pricked, this pony still looks full of running at the end of the 2007 point-to-point.

Opposite page:
Riders assemble at the 1½-mile start of the 2007 Boxing Day Point-to-Point races. Small groups of entrants make up the various race categories.

It is amazing where some ponies will venture in
their search for the tastiest morsels of food!

On New Forest roads, ponies have right of way ... even when they are not moving!

Signboards make handy scratching posts!

Opposite: First rain then freezing cold conditions cooled these ponies during a long winter night. They stood broadside on to catch the warming rays of the early morning sunshine and the water began to evaporate from their coats.

This lip-curling behaviour is most commonly seen during the mating season of the Forests' ponies, not during a drift when this photo was taken.

Head Agister, Jonathan Gerrelli cuts the tail of a pony to
denote in which part of the Forest its owner lives.

A selection of the brands used on the ponies to denote ownership.

A mare leaves the pound after temporary penning at a drift near Turf Hill. Her ownership will have been noted so that the appropriate fee can be paid to the Verderers.

Snow is rare in the New Forest and soon it will melt away and
the ponies will welcome the warmer times.

Head Agister, Jonathan Gerrelli checks the health of a group of ponies.

Commoner, Les Maton
thoughtfully views a group
of penned ponies.

Foals are usually born in April
or May. Here, a mare stands
proudly by as her new youngster
has its picture taken. Beware,
some mares do not like you
getting this close to their offspring.

49

A foal at the Beaulieu Road pony sales in the autumn.

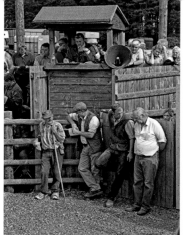

Commoners discuss prices as the auctioneer announces the next pony to be sold.

A pony leaves the selling ring and will soon be in the hands of its new owner.

These ponies will soon return to their favourite haunts once released from the pound at Weirs.

Commoners stand ready to drive ponies towards the pound during a drift.

Opposite page:
Pony drifts take place at high speed and it pays not to get in the way of thundering hooves!

Commoners assess the condition of their own and others' ponies during a drift near Brockenhurst.

Agister Andrew Napthine looks over a pound full of ponies.

Former Head Agister, Brian Ingram cleans and cools his pony at the end of a drift.

Traffic has been halted as a good group of ponies are turned across
a road and towards the pound during a drift near Brockenhurst.

During a drift it is important to try and prevent ponies from reaching the road.

Overleaf: Rider and helpers on foot work together to
turn this mare and foal towards the pound.

Ponies know their home range well enough to avoid a large boggy area even when they are travelling at high speed during a drift.

During the winter months when grass grows less well in the Forest, many ponies are held on the Commoners' own land and given extra food.

Tail markings vary from one Agister's region of the Forest to another. This is the mark for Robert Maton's region of the Forest.

Ponies graze beside the road and the Abbey walls at Beaulieu.

Opposite: This mare and her foal graze the colourful heathland near Ragged Boys Hill.

Glossary

Agister
The 5 New Forest Agisters are Officers of the Verderers. Their work covers a wide range of duties specifically relating to the welfare of the Forest's depastured animals and to the well-being of the Forest itself.

Drift
The act of rounding up ponies and holding them temporarily in a pound.

Pound
The pen used for holding ponies at the end of a drift.

Verderer
There are 5 Verderers appointed by various statutory bodies and 5 elected by the Commoners. They ensure that people exercising their Rights of Pasture do so in a responsible and proper manner. They 'administer' the local by-laws in relation to the management and welfare of the stock and also have control over certain developments within the New Forest.